How To Increase & Release The Anointing

Rodney M. Howard-Browne

How To Increase & Release The Anointing
ISBN 1-884662-03-X
Copyright © 1995 by Revival Ministries International
Printed in the United States of America.

Published by:
RMI Publications
P.O. Box 292888, Tampa, Florida 33687, USA
    Phone: 813-971-9999
    FAX: 813-971-0701
P.O. Box 3900, Randburg 2125, South Africa
P.O. Box 24, Liphook, Hampshire, GU307YX, UK

All scripture quotations are taken from the King James Version of the Bible.

How To Increase & Release The Anointing

Contents

1

Laying The Foundation

I AM ALWAYS AMAZED to see, that whilst a man's desire is to serve God, it seems so easy for him to fall into the rut of religion and tradition. It is equally amazing to me, to see an individual who was in the world, a slave to sin and on their way to a lost eternity without God, receiving salvation and coming into glorious liberty, then a few years later going back into bondage again. This time to religion and a religious system.

We are living in a day and age when man is looking for a formula for everything that he does in life including his walk with the Lord. I am not writing this book to bring out a formula for the anointing, but rather to give some guidelines concerning the anointing and how to operate in the anointing as a lifestyle. Not hype or "Step One, Two and Three," but a relationship with Jesus, 24 hours a day.

A Relationship, Not a Formula

There are several things that we can do to enhance the anointing in our lives. To begin with, the anointing is based upon a relationship, not a formula. This is important to realize, as it is so easy for people to fall into a trap of trying so hard to be used of God, that they open themselves up to a religious spirit.

Many, in their quest for the anointing, are trying to imitate the lifestyle of great men of God. They want to walk their walk and talk their talk, but not out of their own relationship with Jesus. They try to use their imitation of the daily habits of these men as a means to have God's anointing manifest in their lives. Many times then, people end up doing things with the wrong motive. For example, there are those who hold healing meetings so that they can have a crowd, not so that they can get people healed. That's a wrong motive for wanting to see miracles take place.

It also is so easy to be in the habit of seeing someone who is successful, wanting to find out what they are doing, so that we can imitate them, whilst hoping for the same success that they achieved. I remember when I started out in the ministry, I read about Smith Wigglesworth, wanted what he had in God, and so I decided that I would find out what he did and do it. I found out that he would wake up at four o'clock every morning and have communion. Then he would pray for three hours. So I began to do the same, I would get up and begin to pray, but then I would fall asleep after a short while and wake up much later in the morning. I had to realize that it was a relationship, not a formula. Later on, in talking to others, I found out that I was not the only one that had done this. Others had also gone to this extreme, because of the idea that the anointing must be linked to a formula.

This action was based on trusting in a formula and not in a relationship. It is important to realize, that Smith Wigglesworth did not do all of those things in order to have miracles in his life. He had a relationship with the Lord, and then out of this relationship, he ministered and miracles were the result. Later on, I found out that Smith Wigglesworth also never read a newspaper and so for a while I wouldn't read one either only to discover that he couldn't read a newspaper. He was illiterate and learned to read only the Bible.

It is not what you know, it's who you know. Paul prayed for

himself that he might know Jesus more intimately, and that must be our prayer as well. If we read the book of Acts chapter 4 verse 13, we read about Peter and John and we see that the Bible says, "When they saw the boldness of Peter and John, and perceived that they were unlearned and ignorant men, they marveled; and they took knowledge of them, that they had been with Jesus." Can people tell that you have been with Jesus, lately? What Peter and John had, was not based upon a formula, but rather upon their relationship with the Lord Jesus Christ.

A Person, Not a Language

I think one of the biggest problems in many Pentecostal and charismatic circles is that people seek a language, and not the Holy Spirit. Without the realization that the Holy Spirit is a person, how can an individual walk in the presence of the Lord? And how can that individual have a relationship with the Holy Spirit if they think that the Holy Spirit is a language. The Holy Spirit is not a language nor is He a manifestation. He is a **person**. The third person of the Godhead. Jesus said to the disciples, "Tarry ye in the city of Jerusalem, until ye be endued with power from on high" (Luke 24:59).

Some people think He said, "You will receive tongues." Acts 1 verse 8 says, "Ye shall receive power after that the Holy Spirit has come upon you." He never said that you shall receive tongues. What good is tongues without the power? We have many babbling believers today, with very little power. Many who have never been introduced to the person of the Holy Spirit, but to a language or to a manifestation.

When He told them to tarry for the Holy Spirit, they didn't know for whom they were waiting. Jesus did not say, "Whilst you are tarrying at Jerusalem you, will hear a knock at the door at nine o'clock in the morning." If there had come a knock on the door and if someone had walked in and said, "I am the Holy Spirit," I am sure that they would have welcomed that person and said, "Yes, Jesus said You were coming, come inside."

Yet on the day of Pentecost, there came a sound from heaven as of a rushing, mighty wind. There appeared unto them cloven tongues as of fire and it sat upon each of them. They were all filled with the Spirit and began to speak with other tongues, as the Spirit gave them utterance (see Acts 2:1-4).

I want you to notice they were filled, then they spoke. They were filled first. Also, power was evident in their lives. You see, the early church had the substance, but unfortunately, the latter church in most cases, has only the formula. Let's get back to the substance, the tangibility, the heavenly materiality of what the early church had.

Having an Encounter with God

I believe if we desire to be used of God, we need to have an encounter with Him. Paul talked about how he had seen the Lord on the way to Damascus. Moses had a burning bush experience. To be honest with you, so had everyone who has ever been used of God.

Job had an encounter with God at the end of his ordeal. God revealed Himself to Job, asking Job where he was when God laid the foundation of the earth. "Do you have a voice that can thunder like me?" God asked Job (Job 40:9).

Job finally spoke to God. His words speak for many people, I think. He said, "I have heard of thee by the hearing of the ear: but now my eye seeth thee" (Job 42:5). It is one thing to read the Book; it's another thing to meet the Author of the Book.

The Life of Prayer

First of all, what is prayer? Prayer is communication and it's communicated in two directions. In many believers' lives, prayer is a one-sided conversation. They pray, "Give me, give me." They are always asking for something from God.

Prayer, for the believer, should not be a religious ritual performed on a daily basis to attain a certain level of spirituality. It should be a daily fellowship with our heavenly Father, springing out of our love for Him.

We have to realize that we are not under the Old Covenant, but under the New. Whatever is done under the New Covenant must be done out of faith and love. Otherwise, it is nothing more than dead works, something for which we should repent.

A Lifestyle of Prayer

Every believer needs to develop a lifestyle of prayer. The Word says, "Pray without ceasing" (First Thessalonians 5:17). We need to realize that we can live in the spirit of prayer, whereby we pray all the time. Our heart can always be crying out to Him. Our thought life should never be far away from God.

I asked the Lord why some people never feel or sense His touch in their lives. I believe it's because most of their waking moments are caught up in the affairs of this life. Their hearts are far from God.

Jude 20 says, "But ye, beloved, building up yourselves on your most holy faith, praying in the Holy Ghost." It is important to pray in the Spirit and keep yourself built up spiritually. Some people are always saying, "I need to get prayed up." Don't just get prayed up; stay prayed up. Stay in the Spirit.

Different Rules for Different Prayers

We know that just as different sports have different rules, so there are different kinds of prayer and not all prayer has the same rules. For the believer who would be used of God, there are two prayers especially, among all the others, that need to be prayed.

The first prayer is the prayer of consecration. Jesus prayed this prayer in the Garden of Gethsemane. It was a prayer of consecrating His will to do the will of His Father.

The second prayer is the prayer of repentance, whereby we continually keep our hearts right with God. This prayer is not based on the consciousness of sin alone, but springs out of our love for Jesus. That is, we would not want to do anything, in any way, shape, or fashion, to hurt Him.

These two prayers are sadly missing in many lives. For those who desire to have the anointing, they would do well to remember that only a consecrated, yielded, repentant heart will be used of God.

CHAPTER

2

Charismatic Myths

Is God a Captive in His Own Heavens?

THERE ARE THOSE IN THE CHURCH who think that in order to see revival, our prayer life must be directed towards the devil in an attitude of warfare. They believe we must wage war on the devil in the heavens, to release God, so that He can move freely. They act as if God is bound in the heavenly realm, waiting desperately for a believer to loose Him so that the plan and purpose of God can be done on earth.

"Honey, I Blew up the Devil" & Other Nintendo Games

This game of spiritual warfare is nothing more than a spiritual nintendo game played by baby Christians who have no understanding of the fact that Jesus defeated the devil two thousand years ago. He has sent the Holy Ghost to empower the believer and to flow through that individual's life to enforce the devil's defeat.

In this game, the devil is seen through the eyes of the believer as very big and in control. And God is seen as having a problem containing him. Believers now, instead of preaching the gospel which will set the captives free and destroy the yoke of bondage in their lives, are in their closets waging war on the devil. Many live in a fantasy world of spiritual warfare. It's all probably the result of a bad dream from an overdose of pizza with too much cheese.

This has permeated the Church, infiltrated the worship, prayer, and study of the Word to such an extent that when you go to some churches, you wonder who are you going to worship. All they ever seem to do is talk about the devil and pray about what he is doing. The sermon and even their heavenly language is directed towards the devil.

By the end of the service, all the believers are stamping their feet, binding and loosing in a frightened frenzy. It reminds me of a bunch of kids who have been told they are going to have to walk home in the dark past a graveyard after they've just seen a horror movie.

Pulling Down Strongholds — In the Mind or the Heavenlies?

For the weapons of our warfare are not carnal, but mighty through God, to the pulling down of strongholds. Casting down imaginations, and every high thing that exalteth itself against the knowledge of God, and bringing into captivity every thought to the obedience of Christ (Second Corinthians 10:4,5). This speaks of a warfare in the mind of man, rather than in the heavenlies.

We have no account of Paul or anyone else — including Jesus — indulging in these so-called warfare practices. This practice is based on Daniel's 21-day fast while the angel was trying to get through. This, of course, is Old Covenant. The Holy Ghost is here on earth now. He came on the day of Pentecost and never left.

So rather than indulging in religious practices that do not produce any fruit, let us turn to the proclamation of the gospel followed by the demonstration of the power of the Holy Ghost, resulting in the establishment of the kingdom of God on the earth.

"The kingdom is not meat and drink but righteousness, and peace, and joy in the Holy Ghost" (Romans 14:17). This means that the kingdom of God is not a works program which revolves around rules and regulations, but rather a lifestyle in which you do what is right, because God's laws are "written on your heart" (Proverbs 3:3).

It is interesting to note that the greatest soul winners in the world have never indulged in such religious practices. They have spent their time in prayer, fellowshipping with the Lord on a daily basis, and ministering out of an overflow of that communion with Him.

What Did Jesus Do?

When Jesus was tempted of the devil, He did not try to war with him, but instead He answered him with the Word saying, "It is written." When He stood at the tomb of Lazarus and prayed, it was not a prayer of desperation, but rather He prayed out loud for the benefit of those around Him. He turned first toward heaven, speaking only to God, not addressing demonic realms. Then out of His relationship with His heavenly Father, He proclaimed the desired result. (See John 11:41-44.)

Also, in the country of the Gadarenes, the demons knew who Jesus was. They said, "Have you come to torment us before our time?" They knew that their time was not yet and they pleaded with Him to cast them into the swine. He did, not in a three-hour battle, but with one word — go! (See Mark 5:1-14.)

There Is a True Intercession

I am not against true intercession, which is the Holy Ghost praying through us, the perfect will of God for any situation. But I am against fleshly prayer that produces nothing but pride in the

individual's life and robs them of their joy and peace and their pro-
ductivity in the kingdom of God.

A city like Los Angeles, California, is a classic example of a
city that in recent times has been bombarded by prayer in some
form or another. Yet it has seen anything but revival. It has seen
earthquakes, racial rioting, drought, fires, floods, and more. I am
not saying that we will not see revival come to L.A. If and when
it does come, it will not be to the credit or glory of men, but
through the outward working of the Spirit of God through men,
resulting in many won into the kingdom of God. True revival will
touch the hearts of men, bringing them to repentance and salvation. When Jesus is lifted up, He draws all men unto Himself
(John 12:32). The goodness of God leads us to repentance
(Romans 2:4).

Fact or Fiction?

Again, I must emphasize that I am not against true intercession. But remember that the devil realizes he can't stop the Church
from praying. He can, however, get us praying in the wrong direc-
tion. This will result in nothing but dead works, frustrating the
believer. It will cause him to be caught up in a super spiritual world
of warfare and demonic forces, fighting a seemingly never-ending
battle. All this distracts him from doing the works of Jesus —
preaching, teaching, and demonstrating the power of God.

Even if he or she did minister, it would not be with an over-
comer's mentality, seeing the victory purchased at Calvary as a finished work. Instead it is a warfare mentality, seen through the eyes
of a Christian writer's novel. The truth is, Jesus has already won
the war and given us the power and authority.

The Red Rag Mentality

The Church reminds me of a bull in a bullring chasing a red rag, not realizing it is the matador who holds the rag who is the problem. If the bull ever found out the truth, it would be the end of the matador. Even so, the Word of God declares that when the enemy is revealed on that day, many will be amazed. They will say, "Is this the one who did bring kings down?" Many, in the Church, will be astounded.

We need to realize that the devil is defeated. He is not omnipresent and he is a creation, not creator. These simple truths will help us to see clearly that prayer must be used primarily to fellowship with the Lord and to spend time being filled up in His presence. Then out of an overflow of His touch, we minister to the needs of hurting humanity.

3

A Lifestyle —
A Relationship

The Study of the Word of God

PAUL, IN SPEAKING TO TIMOTHY, SAID, "Study to shew thyself approved unto God, a workman that needeth not to be ashamed, rightly dividing the word of truth" (Second Timothy 2:15). Every believer needs to have a workable knowledge of God's Word. One of the problems we face is that many Christians don't even know the basics of the Word. They are caught up in the non-absolutes of the Word. It is not producing life and joy and freedom, but rather death and bondage to man-made doctrines and traditions.

The scripture says many walk after the doctrines of men, "having a form of godliness, but denying the power thereof" (Second Timothy 3:5). That is why Paul admonished Timothy to, "Preach the Word; be instant in season, out of season; reprove, rebuke, exhort with all long-suffering and doctrine. For the time will come when they will not endure sound doctrine; but after their own lusts shall they heap to themselves teachers, having itching ears" (Second Timothy 4:2,3).

Don't Throw Arrows in the Dark

The study of the scripture should be systematic, rightly dividing between the Old and the New and between absolutes and non-absolutes. It is evident that many take a little of the Old Testament and a little of the New Testament and make up their own covenant. It is one that brings them into freedom for a little while and then puts them back into bondage.

I suggest that once a believer has a workable knowledge of the scripture, then he or she should spend time in the Epistles and also the Gospels. We should study the Epistles to find out what is available to us through the finished work of the cross. We should study the Gospels to follow closely the ministry of Jesus and to build into our lives an image of Jesus and His earthly ministry. Jesus said, "He that believeth on me, the works that I do shall he do also; and greater works than these shall he do" (John 14:12).

Any time spent in the Old Testament must be backed up with time spent in the New. Otherwise the student will come out with a picture of negativity and failure, because the Old Testament was only a type and shadow of the New. The Old without the New produces bondage and death. The Old Testament shows us of our need for a Savior. The New Testament shows us the Savior.

The New Testament is the fulfillment of the Old and the completion of everything Jesus came for. That is why He cried, "It is finished," and the veil of the temple was rent in two from top to bottom. The Holy Spirit came out of an earthly tabernacle made with the hands of man, never again to live therein. He now lives in my heart and your heart. Thus the scripture says, "We have this treasure in earthen vessels" (Second Corinthians 4:7).

The Gospel Is Simple

If you do any study on issues, try not to get sidetracked away from the simplicity of the gospel. Do not run off on a tangent into something that does not produce life.

You will always know if you are into false doctrine when you begin to lose your joy and your peace. The scripture says, "In thy presence is fullness of joy; at thy right hand there are pleasures for evermore" (Psalm 16:11). Let peace be your umpire.

Allow the Holy Spirit to lead and guide you in your study of the scripture. Remember that the Holy Spirit is the teacher. He will take God's Word and make it alive for you. The letter kills, but the Spirit gives life.

Having a Hearing Ear

Jesus said, "My sheep hear my voice. The voice of a stranger they will not follow" (see John 10:5,27). It is interesting to find out that many Christians who have a "quiet time" really do have a quiet time, because they never hear from heaven. They never listened to hear God actually speak to them.

"As many as are led by the Spirit of God, they are the sons of God" (Romans 8:14). God will lead you by His Spirit, but there needs to be a sensitivity to the anointing and it only comes with spending time in His presence and listening for His voice. Only then do we recognize when God is speaking to us and instantly obey. In other words, we need to develop a hearing ear.

He That Has Ears to Hear

"He that has ears to hear what the Spirit is saying," is a phrase that is repeated throughout the New Testament. It's not talking about the natural ear, but the spiritual ear.

We know the story of Samuel and how he heard someone calling his name. He went to Eli and said, "You called me." Eli replied, "I did not call you." This happened several times before Eli realized that it was God who was speaking, even though he did not hear the voice (not having ears to hear). He told Samuel, "Go lie down and when you hear the voice, say 'Speak, Lord, for your servant is listening'" (see First Samuel 3:1-10).

Following the Ministry of Jesus

I believe that another way to increase the anointing is to spend much time reading the Gospels and following closely the ministry of Jesus. Jesus said, "The Son can do nothing of himself, but what he seeth the Father do" (John 5:19). I believe we can only do what we see Jesus do.

The disciples followed Jesus observing the signs and wonders and miracles that He did. He said to them, "He that believeth on me, the works that I do shall he do also; and greater works than these shall he do: because I go unto my Father" (John 14:12).

He sent the Holy Ghost to empower them in order for them to go forth and do His works. Later, when Peter and John were taken in front of the chief priests and elders and commanded by them not to preach or teach in the name of Jesus, they said, "We cannot but speak the things which we have seen and heard" (Acts 4:20).

You Will Be Like Those You Hang Around

You will only do the things you have both seen and heard. If you spend time around a ministry that does not believe in healing nor in the power of the Holy Spirit, then you will be just like them.

When people come to me and say, "I don't believe in miracles," or tell me, "Miracles have passed away," I tell them that they have come too late to convince me. I've seen God move. I have seen His power. I believe in miracles.

Something I enjoy doing and which has been a great blessing to me, is reading about the miracles Jesus did, closing my eyes and picturing them in my mind. I imagine myself back in those times, hearing Jesus teach and seeing the miracles that He did.

Looking For a Man — Missing Your Miracle

Let us look at the story of the man Jesus healed at the pool of Bethesda (John 5:1-9). The Bible says, "There was by the sheep market a pool, in the Hebrew tongue called Bethesda, having five porches. In these porches lay a great multitude of blind, halt, and maimed people, waiting for the troubling of the water. At a certain season an angel would come and trouble the water and whoever stepped in first was made whole of whatever disease he had."

If you would for a moment, picture the events that transpired when an angel came down and troubled the water. Imagine how frustrating it must have been for those who had been waiting for years for their miracle. While they were coming, someone else got there ahead of them.

Jesus arrives on the scene and walked up to a man who was powerless to help himself. He asks him a question. "Wilt thou be made whole?" That seems a ridiculous question to ask a man who is sitting by a healing pool waiting for an angel to trouble the water. If he was from New York he might have said, "Of course, I want to be healed. What do you think I am sitting here for, my health?"

Jesus was provoking the man in order to locate his level of faith. The man gave Jesus a ridiculous answer in response to the question. He said, "Sir, I have no man. While I am coming, another steps down and is healed in my place." Jesus didn't ask him if he had a man. He asked him, "Wilt thou be made whole?" In reality, Jesus was saying, "I am your man." And when He told him, "Rise, take up your bed, and walk," the man arose and walked.

Looking for the Missing Pieces of the Puzzle

Anyone reading this passage of scripture could say to me, "Well, Brother Rodney, isn't it wonderful that this man was healed?" Yes, it is wonderful. But when I initially began to study this whole story something bothered me about it that I couldn't put my finger on.

I read and reread this passage of scripture and could not help wondering, why with all those sick people there, did Jesus only heal one of them. I could not understand why others around this man didn't shout out to Jesus and ask Him to come over and heal them as He had healed that man.

When I prayed about it, the answer suddenly dawned on me. It was so simple I could have kicked myself for not seeing it sooner. The reason the others were not healed, was because they had a man to help them get into the pool. They were so busy looking to their man, they missed their miracle. Their miracle came into the midst of them, and then left. They were untouched because they were too focused on the natural realm to see God's power manifested right in front of them.

As we spend time in the Gospels and follow the ministry of Jesus, we will begin to see it without the cloak of religion, and rather in all its power and glory.

CHAPTER

4

Being Faithful To The Call Of God

G OD ANOINTS AND EQUIPS US according to the measure of His call on our lives, but we should remember that the anointing is not taught — it is caught. The only way to get the anointing is to be where the anointing is being poured out. Also, doing what God has called you to do, will cause His power to flow through you.

One of the problems many ministers face is that they get discouraged when things don't go the way they would like. They end up quitting the ministry just prior to their breakthrough.

I believe the Lord is looking for those who will be faithful to obey the call. He will test you in ministry before you see an increase. The scripture says, if you are faithful over little, God will make you a ruler over much.

A Case of the Forgotten Son

The story of David is a wonderful story of a young man whom God had chosen to be king. God had spoken to the prophet Samuel and told him to anoint a king in Saul's place. Samuel went and stood in front of Jesse's sons, but none of them was found suitable for the position of king. God had chosen David because of his faithfulness with a few sheep and the attitude of his heart. Even though he was out with the sheep, God knew where he was and anointed him in Saul's place.

David had been many years in preparation for his calling. He was faithful to take on the lion and the bear. Little did he know that God would have him take on a giant. Many in the ministry today, want the giant, but are not prepared or faithful to take on the lion and the bear. We live in a day and age of instant results. People want to have success and they want it now. Many judge success by monetary gain or other achievements such as a large number of church members, an extensive radio and television ministry, or a huge mailing list.

Success Is Doing What God Has Called You to Do

Success is doing what God has called you to do. I have had the privilege of being around some of the great men of God who pastor large churches. One of them publicly made the statement to other ministers that it didn't matter if you only had 100 people in your church. If that was what God had called you to, then you should be content and happy in that ministry.

Privately I heard him make the statement about a pastor of a small church, "When he gets a thousand people in his church, then let him come and talk to me." In other words, he was saying the man was not worthy to talk to him because he was not in the same league. The public statement he made was the truth, but in his heart he could not have believed it or he would not have made the second statement. God does not see things the same way we do — He measures our success according to our obedience — not simply according to our accomplishments, as men do.

I am reminded of a statement I used to tell the Bible students at a school in South Africa where I lectured several years ago. "Always remember the little man on your way up, because you might need him on your way down."

If the grace of God did not lead you to a certain place, then the grace of God cannot keep you there.

Legends in Their Own Mind

Another minister informed me — comparing his ministry to the ministry of another — that his ministry was a Cadillac and the other was a Yugo. I thought to myself, Then I must be the hubcap on the Yugo. One preacher informed a friend of mine that he was one of the top five speakers in the world today. I thought to myself, I must be one of the bottom five.

It is not what you have done or achieved in man's eyes that counts; it is faithfulness to the call of God. When I stand before my heavenly Father I desire to hear Him say, "Well done, thou good and faithful servant. Enter into the joy of the Lord." I don't want to hear, "Well done, thou good and successful servant. You have already received your reward, it's the praise of men."

The Danger of Forgetting Where You've Come From

When God calls and anoints a person, many times it is just an ordinary individual. The man seemingly rises out of the dust, to achieve greatness in God. Amazingly, later when he is asked what the key to his success is, he gives a ten-point guideline to the secret of his success.

But it had nothing to do with ten points. It was the touch of God in the individual's life which resulted in the call. He remained faithful to fulfill the call and succeeded. He obeyed God and followed His leading on a daily basis. It is as simple as that.

It Doesn't Come Overnight

Success does not come overnight; it is formed in the fires of life. In that crucible, theories become proved and foundations are laid. Usually those who rise overnight, fall before daybreak.

Some look at the success that we've had in the evangelistic field in recent times in the ministry in different parts of the earth (in comparison to others we have not even begun yet), and they say to me, "Your ministry shot up overnight." All I can tell them is that it's been the longest night of my life.

The Importance of Worship

Jesus said, "The hour cometh, and now is, when the true worshippers shall worship the Father in Spirit and in truth: for the Father seeketh such to worship him" (John 4:23). Worship is so important, not just corporately, but also privately. As we begin to worship Him, the presence of the Lord will come upon us.

The scripture says in Psalm 91:1, "He that dwelleth in the secret place of the most High will abide under the shadow of the Almighty." Worship is that secret place. We need to develop a lifestyle of prayer. We need to develop a lifestyle of worship. I know in my own life that worship is a very important part of my walk with the Lord on a daily basis.

Integrity in Life & Ministry

It is very important to be oneself. We are living in a day and age when there is so much pressure to follow the crowd and be an echo instead of being a voice. I believe God wants to raise up voices in these last days. He wants those who will speak as an oracle of God.

There is a lack of integrity in the ministry today. I believe if we would be used of God on a continual basis, we need to develop Godly character in the area of integrity.

We live in a day when men have very little integrity, not only

Masses of people are hungry for God
to touch their lives with His Spirit.

Capacity crowds hav

ded the various revivals in numerous venues all around the world.

Hundreds come to surrender their lives and make Jesus
their Lord and Savior as a result of the preaching of the Word.

in the world but also in the Church. The scripture says, "Who shall ascend into the hill of the Lord? or shall stand in His holy place? He that hath clean hands, and a pure heart" (Psalm 24:3, 4). It is sad to think that in the Church today, there is a lack of integrity. People say whatever they want to say and then forget about it completely. Some even deny that they said or promised anything.

The motto I have adopted in the ministry is, "Expect nothing from anyone, but commit yourself to be a giver." The Bible says, "God will honor a man who swears to his own hurt and changeth not" (Psalm 15:4). Many times when I am promised things from men of God, I don't get excited until I see it happen. It is sad that you cannot trust someone's word. The lack of integrity has plagued the ministry for many years, from the Elmer Gantry of Hollywood to real life, modern day televangelism. Sometimes it is because the gift on the man's life has developed beyond the man's character. Before you pray and ask God to anoint you, ask God to burn His character and nature into you, that the fruit of the spirit would be made manifest in your life and Godly character would be yours. Then the ministry will not be based upon a gift or a manifestation, but upon the Word of God that has become a living reality in your life.

5

The Heart Of Man

Man Looks on the Outside — God Looks on the Heart

And the Lord said unto Samuel, How long wilt thou mourn for Saul, seeing I have rejected him from reigning over Israel? fill thine horn with oil, and go, I will send thee to Jesse the Bethlehemite: for I have provided me a king among his sons.

And Samuel, said, How can I go? if Saul hear it, he will kill me. And the Lord said, Take an heifer with thee, and say, I am come to sacrifice to the Lord.

And call Jesse to the sacrifice, and I will shew thee what thou shalt do: and thou shalt anoint unto me him whom I name unto thee.

And Samuel did that which the Lord spake, and came to Bethlehem. And the elders of the town trembled at his coming, and said, Comest thou peaceably?

And he said, Peaceably: I am come to sacrifice unto the Lord: sanctify yourselves, and come with me to the sacrifice. And he sanctified Jesse and his sons, and called them to the sacrifice.

And it came to pass, when they were come, that he looked on Eliab, and said, Surely the Lord's anointed is before him.

But the Lord said unto Samuel, Look not on his countenance, or on the height of his stature; because I have refused him: for the Lord seeth not as man seeth; for man looketh on the outward appearance, but the Lord looketh on the heart.

Then Jesse called Abinadab, and made him pass before Samuel. And he said, Neither hath the Lord chosen this.

Then Jesse made Shammah to pass by. And he said, Neither hath the Lord chosen this.

Again, Jesse made seven of his sons to pass before Samuel. And Samuel said unto Jesse, The Lord hath not chosen these.

And Samuel said unto Jesse, Are here all thy children? And he said, There remaineth yet the youngest, and, behold, he keepeth the sheep. And Samuel said unto Jesse, Send and fetch him: for we will not sit down till he come hither.

And he sent, and brought him in. Now he was ruddy, and withal of a beautiful countenance, and goodly to look to. And the Lord said, Arise, anoint him: for this is he.

Then Samuel took the horn of oil, and anointed him in the midst of his brethren: and the Spirit of the Lord came upon David from that day forward. So Samuel rose up, and went to Ramah.

1 Samuel 16:1-13

God Uses the Foolish Things to Confound the Wise

I want you to see something about the anointing of God

upon individuals. God doesn't choose whom we would choose. God doesn't look upon a person's qualifications. God doesn't look upon their education. God doesn't look upon their stature. Their abilities in the natural have absolutely nothing to do with His placing His hand upon them.

> **For ye see your calling, brethren, how that not many wise men after the flesh, not many mighty, not many noble, are called:**
>
> **But God hath chosen the foolish things of the world to confound the wise; and God hath chosen the weak things of the world to confound the things which are mighty;**
>
> **And the base things of the world, and things which are despised, hath God chosen, yea, and things which are not, to bring to nought things that are:**
>
> **That no flesh should glory in his presence.**
>
> 1 Corinthians 1:26-29

A New Testament Example

> **But there was a certain man, called Simon, which beforetime in the same city used sorcery, and bewitched the people of Samaria, giving out that himself was some great one:**
>
> **To whom they all gave heed, from the least to the greatest, saying, This man is the great power of God.**
>
> **And to him they had regard, because that of long time he had bewitched them with sorceries.**
>
> **But when they believed Philip preaching the things concerning the kingdom of God, and the name of Jesus Christ, they were baptized, both men and women.**
>
> **Then Simon himself believed also: and when he was**

baptized, he continued with Philip, and wondered, beholding the miracles and signs which were done.

Now when the apostles which were at Jerusalem heard that Samaria had received the word of God, they sent unto them Peter and John:

Who, when they were come down, prayed for them, that they might receive the Holy Ghost:

(For as yet he was fallen upon none of them: only they were baptized in the name of the Lord Jesus.)

Then laid they their hands on them, and they received the Holy Ghost.

And when Simon saw that through the laying on of the apostles' hands the Holy Ghost was given, he offered them money,

Saying, Give me also this power, that on whomsoever I lay hands, he may receive the Holy Ghost.

But Peter said unto him, Thy money perish with thee, because thou hast thought that the gift of God may be purchased with money.

Thou hast neither part nor lot in this matter: for thy heart is not right in the sight of God.

Repent therefore of this thy wickedness, and pray God, if perhaps the thought of thine heart may be forgiven thee.

For I perceive that thou art in the gall of bitterness, and in the bond of iniquity.

Then answered Simon, and said, Pray ye to the Lord for me, that none of these things which ye have spoken come upon me.

Acts 8:9-20

Character & The Fruit of the Spirit

Character is a subject that is not discussed in many circles today, but there are certain problems which can arise when a ministry grows too fast. In other words, the anointing upon the person's life develops faster than the character of that individual. Ten or twenty years down the line, their lives blow up and their ministry comes to nothing, because they didn't allow their character to develop.

They didn't walk in the fruit of the Spirit. They didn't walk in love. They didn't walk in the joy of the Lord. They didn't work on their marriage. They didn't take care of their children. Their children end up backsliding away from God. They end up in a divorce because they did not make sure that they had a solid foundation.

Counting the Cost

"No one builds a tower unless he counts the cost" (Luke 14:28). Do you realize the cost of being involved in the ministry? Ministry seems glamorous, but have you counted the cost? What price will you have to pay to walk in that place of serving God?

When I started in the ministry, I was, as they say in the military, gung-ho. I was ready for anything. If God wanted me to run an arctic expedition and preach to the Eskimos I would have done it. I was ready to go at the drop of a hat, without ever finding out what it entailed. Sometimes it is good to be that way, because if you knew what was coming up, you might not go in the first place.

I am reminded of when the Gulf War was on and the young men were going to the Persian Gulf. Different age groups were going. There were the eighteen-year-olds, just out of basic training, who had watched several Rambo movies, and who seemed more than eager to face the enemy. Then there were the guys who were twenty years older, who had been through wars like the Vietnam War. They understood first hand the harsh realities of combat, and they were going out of a different sense of duty. They did not seem as eager, but were probably more committed.

The young man didn't know what he was getting himself into. The first time he dived in a fox hole with mortars flying over his head, he would suddenly realize he was in the middle of war. The older man knew what the commitment was, because he had already faced the heat of the battle.

Coming Ready or Not

When you first enlist in God's army, you may not know what this step entails. You might have said, "Lord, I'm ready for this." That is the way I was. I would pray, "Lord, I'm ready for that. Lord, I'm ready to go here. Lord, I'm ready to do this."

The Lord said, "Rodney, sit down and be quiet." I would get upset and complain, but the Lord would say to me, "You are not ready."

Then you might go through several years of saying, "I'm not ready, Lord, I'm not ready, I'm not ready." The Lord comes to you and says, "Now, Rodney, go and do that."

"O God, I'm not ready!"

He says, "Yes, you are."

You see, four or five years ago, you were ready in your own ability, but now you know you can't do it in your own ability. So you are ready in His ability. When we are not ready in our ability, when we feel the weakest, that is the time when the Spirit of God can rest the strongest upon us.

CHAPTER

6

Total Dependence Upon God

When I Am Weak Then I Am Strong

LIKE THE APOSTLE PAUL SAID, "When I am weak, then I am strong" (Second Corinthians 12:10). He was able to say this in the middle of trials and tribulations. Paul had a thorn in the flesh, which was not sickness nor disease, but was persecution. Everywhere he went in his life and ministry, he was either shipwrecked, beaten, left for dead, spent time in jail, spent a night and a day in the deep — he always had troubles and persecutions on a regular basis.

Paul prayed, "Lord, remove this thing from me." Some people think he got rid of it. No, he didn't. The Lord said to him, "No, I'm not going to remove it from you. My grace is sufficient for you. My anointing is sufficient for you. My ability is sufficient for you to bear this persecution."

So Paul said, "Most gladly therefore will I rather glory in my infirmities, that the power of Christ may rest upon me" (Second Corinthians 12:9). He didn't say anything about sickness. The word "infirmities" here can be translated "weaknesses." He said, "I will rejoice in my infirmities and my weaknesses that the power of Christ may rest upon me." Remember that the Lord sent Ananias to Saul to tell him the things he would suffer for the name of Jesus.

What Are You Made Of?

It is in that hard place, in the beginning of your ministry that you see what you are made of. A grape does not produce juice until it is squeezed. You cannot have grape juice and wine, until you squeeze the grape. Some people need to go through a little bit of pressure in order to produce. Sometimes they get into trouble because of their own stupidity. At other times, the hard place is where they develop character.

The Bible says God tested Abraham. Also in Jesus' ministry He was led by the Holy Ghost into the wilderness to be tempted of the devil. Some people don't understand how it is possible that the Holy Spirit will do that. But God wants to see what you are made of before He entrusts something greater to you.

Nebuchadnezzar learned what the three Hebrew boys were made of when he put them in the burning, fiery furnace. They found out what Daniel was made of when they put him in the lions' den.

You Have to Start at ABC to Get to XYZ

So many people want to be at point Z, but they won't start at A. Until you are ready for ABC, you can't get to XYZ. Be faithful with the little God gives you. It might take five, ten, twenty, thirty or forty years to see it come to pass, but have the stickability.

Stay with what God has called you to do, irrespective of the rain, the sun, the snow, the winter, the summer, the spring, or the adversity, trials, tribulations, and heartaches. Remain constant. Operate in the fruit of patience and continue in what God has called you to do. It will be a process of time and of change, but God will move you into a place where the ministry will come forth into maturity.

Kathryn Kuhlman went through hell and back before her

great ministry was born. She experienced many failures and many hours of loneliness. She said that she knew the day and time when Kathryn Kuhlman died.

Many people think they are out there and no one recognizes them, but God knows and He sees. He looks upon the heart. He is looking for a yielded and a willing vessel.

There Is a Time to Come Forth

It is almost like a lady who becomes pregnant. She would love to have the baby immediately, because it will save her a lot of problems. We have had three children. I've been with my wife during every birth. So I know what my wife went through. It would have been much easier to have all three at one time. It would have taken nine months instead of twenty-seven.

As much as that lady wants to have her baby, she has to wait for the time for the baby to come forth. When a baby is born prematurely, it must be placed in an incubator in intensive care. In the case of extremely premature babies, their lungs are underdeveloped and the child has less chance of surviving.

It is the same with ministries. People have tried to give birth to a ministry prematurely and it doesn't last long. It will last a year, two years, or perhaps five years, and then fade away into nothingness.

Two Kinds of Ministries

There are two kinds of ministries in the earth today. There are the shooting star ministries that will come in a blaze of glory and disappear or blow up. Then there are the ministries that are solid, like the North Star. They will stand the storms of life. They will stand when everything else around is falling, when other ministries are quitting, when people are pulling out of the ministry, when the persecution gets hot. They will stand when they clamp down even more on the television preachers, when they mock the preachers in the newspapers and the media.

These are men of God who will say, "We are not going to compromise! We'll not back down on the healing ministry! We are not going to back down on casting out devils! We are going to arise and boldly proclaim the Word of God in Jesus' name! It doesn't matter if they end up locking us in jail. It doesn't matter if we go to a foreign field and we give our lives there. Let it be so. We will obey the call of God!" These are the kind of people God is looking for.

7

How To Release The Anointing

I T IS ONE THING TO BE ANOINTED OF GOD. It is another thing to be in a position to release that anointing to others, seeing their lives touched with the reality of that heavenly materiality.

After the encounter I had with the Lord in July of 1979, I made plans to go into the full-time ministry. In January of 1980, at the age of eighteen, I joined a group that traveled our nation, ministering in Word and music in many of the nominal mainline denominations across our country.

The group that I joined was interdenominational, but noncharismatic in their beliefs. They frowned upon the Pentecostal experience, but I felt led of the Lord to work with the vehicle they were providing me to spread the gospel. I knew that at anytime I could have been given the left foot of fellowship, because I held fast to my Pentecostal experience.

The Day My Ministry Changed

I can remember the day it first happened — a day my life and ministry changed. It was a day like any other. The interesting thing was, that I was not doing anything that you might think I should have been doing, to cause this to happen. I believe it was all in the plan of God.

We were preaching in a Methodist church. I was back in the vestibule — which is a holy name for a plain, old office — preparing for the service. One of the young ladies on our team came into the office and asked me to pray for her, because she was in terrible pain. I stood up from the chair upon which I was sitting and lifted my right hand, as I normally would, to lay hands upon her and pray. Unexpectedly, the most amazing thing happened.

Hey, This One's Loaded!

I got my hand halfway to her head, almost like a gunslinger would draw a gun out of a holster and point it at his opponent. Suddenly, it felt like my finger tips came off. I felt a full volume of the anointing flow out of my hand. The only way I can explain it is to liken it to a fireman holding a fire hose with a full volume of water flowing out of it. The anointing went out of me, right into her. It looked like someone had hit her on the head with an invisible baseball bat and she fell to the floor.

I was left standing there, totally dumbstruck by what had happened, looking at my hand and at the young lady. I was still conscious of the presence of God flowing out of me, but I was amazed at what had just transpired. About that time, the rest of the team walked in the door. I prayed for them and they all fell out under the power of God.

After a while, I managed to sober them up. I was afraid the priest would walk in through the door and I would have some explaining to do. We moved into the sanctuary and the service began. I was so overwhelmed by the experience and what I had witnessed that I couldn't get it out of my mind.

Call All Those Who Want a Blessing

I began to talk to the Lord all the while as I spoke in the

service. I was asking Him what we (notice I said we) were going to do about what had happened. After all, I was not allowed to talk about the Holy Spirit, speaking in tongues, or falling under the power. But they didn't realize, when you talk about Jesus, the Holy Spirit comes along to find out who you are speaking about.

Here I am, having a conversation with the Lord, asking Him what are we going to do. Suddenly He says to me, "Call all those who want a blessing."

Now, I was in a Methodist church. If you ask a question like that, the whole church will respond. And respond they did. Let us keep in mind that I had said nothing about the Holy Spirit, speaking in tongues, or falling under the power.

They came and stood in one line across the front of the church. The Lord then said to me, "Don't lay both of your hands upon them." We have a problem with folks who are under the impression that ministers are pushing people over. Some do, but that does not detract from the reality that people fall down under the power of God, whether a man has touched them or not. It is the anointing, transferred by the laying on of hands which does the work — not a quick shove. The Lord said to me, "Just lay one finger of your right hand on the forehead of each individual and say, "In the name of Jesus."

I walked over to the first person and said, "In the name of Je..." I did not even have time to say, "sus," when the power of God threw that person to the floor. I went down the line and everyone went out under the power in the same way. They hit the floor just as if someone had slammed them in the head with a Louisville Slugger.

This Is That

Many of them, the moment they hit the floor, began to speak with other tongues as the Spirit gave them utterance. Others were pinned to the floor for up to one and a half hours. I turned and looked at the priest and said anxiously, "It wasn't me. It wasn't me."

As people began to get off the floor, they would come to me and ask the question, "What is this?" I answered them and said, "This is that." They then said, "This is what?" I quoted Acts 2:16-17, "This is that which was spoken by the prophet Joel; And it shall come to pass in the last days, saith God, I will pour out of my Spirit upon all flesh." They remarked, "Oh, is that what it is?"

This experience, to say the least, totally overwhelmed me. The anointing that I had tangibly felt stayed on me, manifesting in that way for about two weeks and then it subsided. It did not leave altogether, but did not manifest in the same way anymore.

This disturbed me. I began to pray and ask the Lord what I could do to get that anointing in full manifestation again in my life. I must be honest with you. For a young man, just beginning in the ministry, this was a totally overwhelming experience. It was something that changed my life and the course of my ministry. It was something that I will never forget as long as I live.

I now began to want the anointing to manifest on people's lives just as I had witnessed it. I wanted to know from the Lord what I might do to have the anointing return in that fashion. I suppose I was looking for a formula — something I could do to get that anointing back in the way I had experienced it.

It's All Me & Nothing to Do with You

The Lord began to instruct me during times of prayer. The first thing He said to me was this: "Son, this anointing is all Me and has nothing to do with you." He said that it was as He wills, not as I will.

The Lord then said to me, "You are just a vessel through

which I am flowing. You cannot earn this anointing; it's given as I will. If I gave you a key and you could get this anointing at anytime, you would begin to think it's all you and not Me. Because you know it is Me that is doing this, you will have to give Me all the glory."

Then I asked Him when I could see this anointing in my life. He told me, "This is a shadow of what is to come. Be faithful in that which I have called you to do. In the process of time, you will walk in it." He told me if He gave it to me now, I would be like a four-year-old with a shotgun. I would blow everything up, including myself.

After this, I continued my study along the lines of the anointing. I closely studied the Gospels and the book of Acts, looking at the ministry of Jesus and the apostles. Then I began to get in as many meetings as I could where mighty men of God were being used of the Lord. I would watch and learn.

8

The Woman With The Issue Of Blood

The Scripture that Became a Reality to Me

A PASSAGE OF SCRIPTURE that has meant so very much to me on the subject of the transference of the anointing is Mark 5:25-34. It is a passage which I believe is the greatest scripture on the subject of the anointing in the entire Word of God.

> And a certain woman, which had an issue of blood twelve years,
>
> And had suffered many things of many physicians, and had spent all that she had, and was nothing bettered, but rather grew worse,
>
> When she had heard of Jesus, came in the press behind, and touched his garment.
>
> For she said, If I may touch but his clothes, I shall be whole.
>
> And straightway the fountain of her blood was dried up; and she felt in her body that she was healed of that plague.
>
> And Jesus, immediately knowing in himself that virtue had gone out of him, turned him about in the press, and said, Who touched my clothes?

And his disciples said unto him, Thou seest the multitude thronging thee, and sayest thou, Who touched me?

And he looked round about to see her that had done this thing.

But the woman fearing and trembling, knowing what was done in her, came and fell down before him, and told him all the truth.

And he said unto her, Daughter, thy faith hath made thee whole; go in peace, and be whole of thy plague.

Mark 5:25-34

The Touch of Faith

We see in this passage of scripture that this woman was in dire straits. She had spent all her money, going to doctors over a twelve-year period, and was not getting any better but was getting worse. Then she heard of Jesus. "She said, If I may touch but his clothes, I shall be made whole. And straightway the fountain of her blood was dried up; and she felt in her body she was healed of that plague" (Mark 5:28, 29).

Something interesting is that she was, first of all, unlawfully touching Jesus. Under the law, anyone with an issue of blood found in a public place, could be taken out and stoned. I guess she had weighed the consequences of being caught and decided that enough is enough. She had to touch the hem of His garment. You can almost hear her saying to herself, "I will sneak my healing, and no one will know about it."

Jesus, that day, was on His way to Jairus' house. The Bible says that a multitude was thronging Him. If the Bible says a multitude was thronging Him, it could have been anywhere from one to ten thousand people.

So one thing is certain. In a crowd such as this, Jesus must have been bumped or touched by the multitudes. Yet something happened only when this woman touched the hem of His garment. Divine virtue or power, called "dunamis" in the Greek, flowed out of Jesus into her body and she was healed.

Placing a Demand on the Anointing

There were many others who must have touched Him that day as He was walking among the crowd. Yet this woman got healed. It was because she placed a demand on the anointing on the life and ministry of Jesus. I want you to know that dunamis, or virtue, flowed into the woman. She felt it flow into her and Jesus felt it flow out of Him. The anointing was tangible and it will always flow into an individual who places a demand upon it.

Her faith was in touching the hem of His garment. When she touched Him, she made the connection and was made whole. There are many other references to people touching Jesus and being healed. In the book of Acts, when the shadows of the apostles passed over the sick, they were healed.

Methods & Results

It is important to realize that the anointing flowing through different ministers might come through different methods. I get a little tired with preachers who criticize methods of the transfer of the anointing. For example, someone said to me that he didn't agree with an evangelist who blew on people. I said, "What's wrong with blowing on people?"

Jesus spat on people. He also breathed on them and said "Receive ye the Holy Ghost" (John 20:22). It's all a point of contact at which time a person can release their faith.

There are many examples of this in the Bible, from anointing oil in James 5:14, to anointed handkerchiefs and aprons in

Acts 19:11, 12. Namaan dipped seven times in the river Jordan for his healing. After making clay with spittle and placing it on a man's eyes, Jesus told him to go and wash in the pool of Siloam. An angel was used to trouble the water at the pool of Bethesda. A brazen serpent was raised in the wilderness for healing. The Bible is full of examples of different, unusual methods used to get results.

One time Moses struck the rock, the other time he was supposed to speak to it. What about Saul trying to get David to wear his armor? David decided to go with his slingshot because it was proven. Too often, we think ours is the only method, but it isn't.

God Is a God of Diversity

Anyone that has been a student of church history will see that God uses ordinary people, but they have different methods. Thank God that we are not all the same. Thank God for diversity.

It makes me think of two mountain climbers, climbing the same mountain from two different sides, both convinced they are the only climbers on the mountain. But you can imagine the shock when they both reach the summit at the same time.

Why should we argue over methods? Let's look at the fruit of the ministry. Jesus said, "Every tree is know by his own fruit" (Luke 6:44). In studying revivals of old, we find that God used different folks with different strokes to get the job done. The sooner we realize this, the sooner we will be able to recognize and respect the touch of God in others' lives.

To Disagree Without Being Disagreeable Is Not Compromise — It's Maturity

I will be honest with you. There are ministers who I don't personally agree with. But I will tell you I know beyond a shadow of a doubt that the hand of the Lord is upon their lives. I rejoice that many lives are being touched by the power of God through their ministries. You have to be spiritually closed not to see that God is using them, even if you don't agree one hundred percent with their teachings or the way they look at things. If we can agree to disagree, we can all climb the mountain together. I made a decision that I will not compromise. It does not matter what anyone says. I will not turn my back upon what I have received from the Lord Jesus. I have spent many hours with men of reputation, privately over the years, checking my heart and my understanding of God's Word so that I would not run in vain.

When I get up to speak I can do so with boldness, knowing that I am not standing alone and that there is nothing new under the sun. That which God is doing through our ministry, He has done from the book of Acts, until the present. I want to encourage you the reader to get hungry for God. I believe that we are at this moment in time seeing one of the greatest moves of God in the earth. Right now it's upon us. I believe that Jesus is getting the church ready. He is coming soon, but before He does, the church is rising up to be the church. The church is going to be the church. And nothing will stand in its way as God's will is done on the earth.

Biography

Dr. Rodney M. Howard-Browne is President and Founder of Revival Ministries International. RMI, as it is commonly known, is a ministry that crosses denominational boundaries and geographical borders to fulfill what the Lord has called it to do — to stir up the Church, telling her to get ready for the coming revival.

In December 1987, Rodney Howard-Browne, along with his wife, Adonica, and their three children, Kirsten, Kelly and Kenneth, moved to the United States to be a part of what the Lord had told Rodney in a word of prophecy. The Lord said, "As America has sown missionaries over the last 200 years, I am going to raise up people from other nations to come to the United States of America." He also said that He was sending a mighty revival to America.

Rodney and his family have been traveling as missionaries in North America, Africa, Europe, Asia, Australia, New Zealand and the United Kingdom.

Revival meetings conducted by Rodney Howard-Browne last from one to four weeks and are reminiscent of revivals of the past, with unusual and powerful demonstrations of the Holy Spirit in every meeting. Salvations, rededications, water baptisms, and baptisms in the Holy Spirit are often accompanied by miracles, signs and wonders.